SPC... ..
Wildflowers

Camilla de la Bedoyere

Miles KeLLY

First published in 2011 by Miles Kelly Publishing Ltd
Harding's Barn, Bardfield End Green, Thaxted, Essex, CM6 3PX, UK

2 4 6 8 10 9 7 5 3 1

Publishing Director Belinda Gallagher
Creative Director Jo Cowan
Editor Amanda Askew
Designer Kayleigh Allen
Production Manager Elizabeth Collins
Reprographics Stephan Davis, Ian Paulyn

ISBN 978-1-84810-445-7

Printed in China

British Library Cataloguing-in-Publication Data
A catalogue record for this book is available from the British Library

ACKNOWLEDGEMENTS
All images are from the Miles Kelly Archives

Made with paper from a sustainable forest

www.mileskelly.net
info@mileskelly.net

www.factsforprojects.com

Self-publish your
children's book

buddingpress.co.uk

CONTENTS

Tick the circles when you have spotted the species.

SEASON WATCH

Wildflowers have life cycles. These are affected by the changes in the weather that each season brings. Most flowers start to bloom in the spring and die when the weather turns colder in winter.

Spring
In spring the soil and air warm up, and the days get longer. Many wildflower plants begin to make an appearance, even if they don't bloom yet. The first sign of new flowers is green shoots sprouting from the ground.

Summer
Colourful blooms contain sweet nectar that attracts insects to them. The insects will help to fertilize the plant by transferring pollen to the ovaries. Once the tiny ovules inside are fertilized, the ovaries can ripen to form seed cases.

Autumn
Blooms die, but seed cases continue to grow, either drying out or wrapped in soft flesh, such as berries. They may fall to the ground, get eaten or be blown away by the wind. Leaves lose their colour, and fall or wither.

Winter
Annual plants die, often when the first frosts bite. Perennial plants are dormant, or rest, over winter. There may be no sign of life, but their roots remain alive, underground, waiting for spring. Some plants flower early and burst through the January snow.

PARTS OF A FLOWER

A **flower develops inside a bud.** Within the petals is a ring of male parts (stamens). Each has a filament topped by an anther containing the male reproductive cells inside pollen grains. At the centre of the flower are the female parts – the stigma and the style. The style widens at its base into an ovary, containing the female reproductive cells in their ovules (eggs).

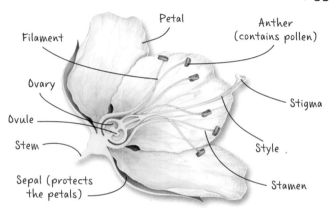

Petal

Anther (contains pollen)

Filament

Ovary

Stigma

Ovule

Stem

Style

Sepal (protects the petals)

Stamen

Pollination and fertilization

When an anther releases its pollen, some grains travel to the stigma (1). The pollen grain grows a tube down the style and into the ovary (2). The tip of the pollen tube then breaks open, releasing a male nucleus, which joins with the female nucleus of the ovule, or egg (3). This joining together is called fertilization, and the new cell that forms is the start of a seed (4).

Fruit and seeds

After fertilization, the ovule turns into a seed and the ovary turns into a fruit. The fruit may become brightly coloured so it is eaten, or dry up and form parachutes or wings to enable it to be blown away.

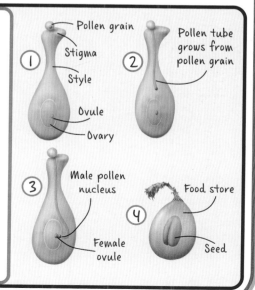

Pollen grain

Stigma

Style

Ovule

Ovary

Pollen tube grows from pollen grain

Male pollen nucleus

Female ovule

Food store

Seed

BINDWEED

The white, trumpet-shaped flowers attract pollinating insects. Bindweed is a weed that grows widely, climbing up fences and plants, gradually smothering them. Bindweed can also spread by seed and is almost impossible to remove. Even a tiny piece of root can grow into a new plant.

ACTUAL SIZE

Bindweed roots are fleshy and white. They grow extensively underground, and may grow down 5 m or more, making it very difficult to get rid of the weed.

FACT FILE

Scientific name
Convolvulus arvensis
Type Bindweed family
Height 50–200 cm
Flowers May to September
Fruit Seeds, August to October

Long, white
flower buds

Trumpet-shaped,
scented flowers

Large, heart-shaped,
green leaves

Green outer
leaves protect
flower bud

Twining,
slender stems

CHAMOMILE

This daisy-like plant is best known for its delicious scent, which is like a mixture of apples and bubblegum. Chamomile used to be widespread, but many of its natural habitats have been destroyed. It is now found growing wild in only a few places in the south of England, especially the New Forest.

ACTUAL SIZE

Chamomile often grows as a ground-covering plant, and is used to create chamomile lawns, which release their scent when walked on.

FACT FILE

Scientific name
Chamaemelum nobile

Type Daisy family

Height Up to 25 cm

Flowers June to August

Fruit Small seeds

One flowerhead on each stalk

Large yellow disc contains many florets

Flower is about 2 cm across

Petals dip down

Grey-green feathery leaves

DAISY

These tiny white flowers are often regarded as weeds. The name, daisy, comes from 'day's eye' because the flower opens like an eye when the sun comes out. Daisies attract pollinating insects, such as bees and hoverflies. Their leaves are hairy and shaped like spoons, and the attractive flowers grow out of the centre of the plant. The plants survive cold and wet winters, and small, white flowers may appear all year round. The flowers grow upwards, facing the sun.

ACTUAL SIZE

FACT FILE

Scientific name *Bellis perennis*
Type Daisy family
Height 2–10 cm
Flowers All year round
Fruit Tiny seeds, after flowering

Dried daisy flowers are used in traditional remedies for treating coughs and colds, diseases of the joints and minor wounds.

Underside of petals are tinged with deep pink

Small, oval-shaped petals surround yellow disc

Straight, 'hairy' stem

GARLIC MUSTARD

A biennial plant, garlic mustard grows in a variety of habitats, but thrives in chalky soils. It can tolerate shady positions and spreads rapidly. The plant can be found throughout the UK, although it is less common in northern Scotland and Ireland. Each upright stem has clusters of small, snow-white flowers at the top and toothed pale-green leaves spiralling along its length.

ACTUAL SIZE

Garlic mustard is an important food plant for the caterpillars of orange tip butterflies.

FACT FILE

Scientific name
Alliaria petiolata
Type Wild cabbage family
Height Up to 1 m
Flowers Mid-March to May
Fruit Small, black seeds

Small, snow-white flowers grow in clusters at the top of the stem

Each flower has four petals

Leaves are triangular with toothed edges

MEADOWSWEET

This wildflower has a strong perfume. It has clouds of whitish flowers on tall stems. Meadowsweet is popular with flying insects, and grows by fresh water and in other damp places throughout Britain and Ireland. Long ago, the blooms were scattered over floors to make a house smell sweet.

ACTUAL SIZE

Meadowsweet keeps blooming throughout the whole summer, providing food for many insects. Its sweet nectar particularly attracts butterflies and bees.

FACT FILE

Scientific name
Filipendula ulmaria
Type Rose family
Height Up to 125 cm
Flowers June to September
Fruit Small, twisted seeds

Flower is about 5 mm across

Creamy-white flowers

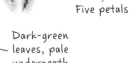

Five petals

Dark-green leaves, pale underneath

Hairless, reddish stems

OXEYE DAISY

Common in meadows, the bright, bold flowerheads of oxeye daisies catch the eye. They grow from year to year, and spread widely to create a carpet of green, topped with white-and-yellow flowerheads. Common daisies look similar to these flowers, but they have smooth, oval leaves and only grow to about 10 cm in height.

ACTUAL SIZE

Fritillary butterflies flock to oxeye daisies in summer. Their wings have orange-brown markings on the upper surfaces, and paler undersides.

FACT FILE

Scientific name
Leucanthemum vulgare
Type Daisy family
Height 10–80 cm
Flowers May to September
Fruit Small seeds

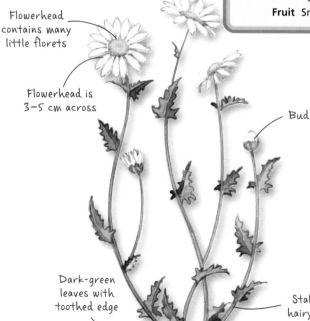

Flowerhead contains many little florets

Flowerhead is 3–5 cm across

Bud

Dark-green leaves with toothed edge

Stalks may be hairy or smooth

SEA KALE

Often found on shingle beaches, sea kale can survive in the dry parts of the upper shore, in pebbly and sandy places. Its thick leaves are able to store water, and a waxy coating on their surfaces stops too much water evaporating. Sea kale rarely flowers before reaching five years of age.

ACTUAL SIZE

This plant used to be steamed and eaten, but now it is rare, and should never be picked.

FACT FILE

Scientific name
Crambe maritima
Type Cabbage family
Height Up to 100 cm
Flowers From June to August
Fruit Round, green fruits

Waxy coating on the leaves

Large, thick leaves, green or purple

Plant grows in a dome shape

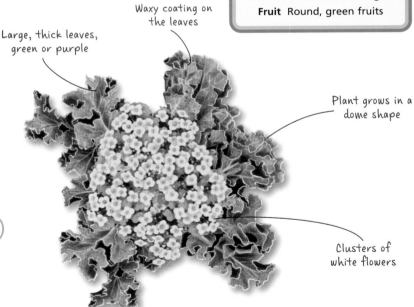

Clusters of white flowers

SNOWDROP

Many snowdrops in the countryside have escaped from gardens and become established in the wild. They are found in damp woods, by streams and in meadows. In sheltered places in southwest England, snowdrops may flower as early as Christmas time. Snowdrops flower early in the year using energy stored in underground bulbs. Wild snowdrops have only one flower per stem and green tips on the inner petals.

ACTUAL SIZE

Snowdrops were probably introduced to the UK from central Europe in Medieval times and are rarely found in Ireland.

FACT FILE

Scientific name
Galanthus nivalis

Type Amaryllis family

Height 15–25 cm

Flowers Late December to March

Fruit Many small seeds

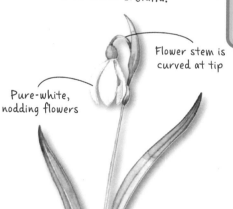

Flower stem is curved at tip

Pure-white, nodding flowers

Narrow, blue-green leaves grow from base of the plant

Three inner petals are short, notched and green at tip

WATER-PLANTAIN

You can see the flowers of this plant best in the afternoon, because they are only open between midday and evening every day. Water-plantain is a stout plant that grows on the edges of watery habitats, especially ponds. It is found everywhere, except northern Scotland.

ACTUAL SIZE

Water-plantain makes a good resting spot for dragonflies and damselflies. Its roots provide safe hiding places for small fish, beetles and insect larvae.

FACT FILE

Scientific name
Alisma plantago-aquatica
Type Water-plantain family
Height Up to 100 cm
Flowers June to September
Fruit Green, small and nut-like

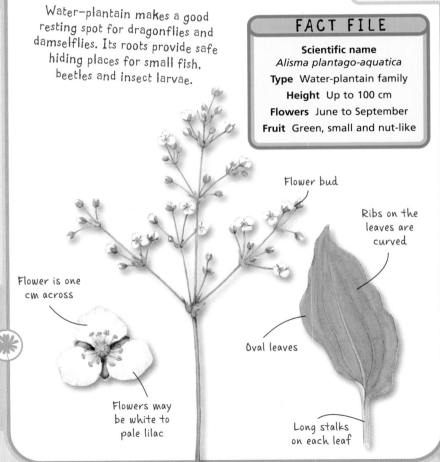

Flower bud

Ribs on the leaves are curved

Flower is one cm across

Oval leaves

Flowers may be white to pale lilac

Long stalks on each leaf

WOOD ANEMONE

Before many trees have unfurled their leaves, wood anemones come into flower in spring, decorating woodland floors. These flowers are able to move towards the light, so they follow the sun as it moves through the sky. Although they have a slight scent, wood anemones do not contain nectar, so insects visiting the flowers may leave hungry.

ACTUAL SIZE

Wood anemones are found in the same habitats as bluebells, which also come into flower during spring.

FACT FILE

Scientific name
Anemone nemorosa

Type Buttercup family

Height Up to 30 cm

Flowers March and April

Fruit Clusters of seeds on old flowerhead

Each flower has five to ten petals

Petals (which are actually sepals) have a pinkish hue

Flower is about 2.5 cm across

Long stalks on leaves

Each leaf has three lobes

BROAD-LEAVED HELLEBORINE

The broad-leaved helleborine is a striking plant, with a single spike that grows tall, bearing up to 100 flowers. Its delicately coloured petals are similar to those of other orchids, and are perfectly shaped to put pollen on the back of any visiting bees. Wasps can be seen feeding on the nectar, and ants often climb into the cup-shaped flowers.

ACTUAL SIZE

Red helleborines usually grow in shady places. These wildflowers are extremely rare, and are found in only a few places in southern England.

FACT FILE

Scientific name
Epipactis helleborine
Type Orchid family
Height Up to 90 cm
Flowers July to September
Fruit Pear-shaped

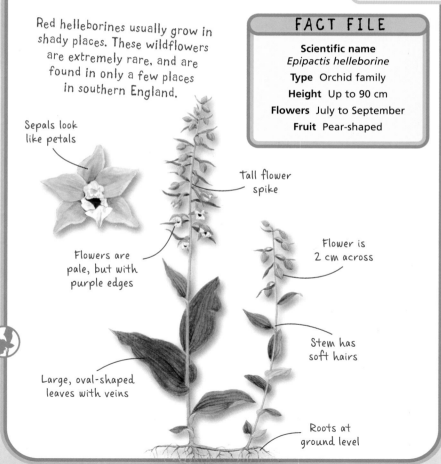

Sepals look like petals

Tall flower spike

Flowers are pale, but with purple edges

Flower is 2 cm across

Stem has soft hairs

Large, oval-shaped leaves with veins

Roots at ground level

LORDS AND LADIES

The flowers of a lords and ladies plant produce a strong, unpleasant smell that attracts insects, which crawl into the flowerheads looking for nectar. As they search, the insects rub against the pollen in the male flowers, and fertilize the female ones. Insects may get trapped and die, and their bodies can be seen in the spathe.

SCALE

If the spathe is cut open the flowers can be seen growing on the spadix. The female flowers are at the base and darker male flowers grow just above them.

FACT FILE

Scientific name
Arum maculatum

Type Arum family

Height Up to 50 cm

Flowers April and May

Fruit Red berries

Thick leaf, called a spathe, which protects the growing flower

Flower-bearing stalk, called the spadix

Spadix is 5 cm tall

Poisonous red berries

Stiff, upright stem

Large, arrow-shaped leaves

BEE ORCHID

There are around 40 members of the wild orchid family in England and Wales, and bee orchids are one of the best known and most widespread of them. Each stem holds between two and seven flowers, and each flower looks as if a fat bumblebee has settled on it. Bee orchids are probably extinct in Scotland.

ACTUAL SIZE

The lower petal of this orchid looks like a bee. Male bees are attracted to it, and as they settle on the flower their backs are coated in pollen.

FACT FILE

Scientific name *Orphrys apifera*

Type Orchid family

Height Up to 30 cm

Flowers June and July

Fruit Long and green with ridges

Bud

Upper petals are rolled, like cylinders, often green or brown

Central lobe of lower petal feels like velvet

Leaves are pointed and slender

Leafy stem

CROSS-LEAVED HEATH

This evergreen plant keeps its leaves all year round. They are arranged in a circle, called a whorl, around the stem. Cross-leaved heath has pretty pink flowers, which hang like bells. They stay on the plant until late summer, making a colourful display in boggy places, and attract bees.

ACTUAL SIZE

Heathers such as the cross-leaved heath tend to keep their leaves over winter. Their flowers are usually small and bell-like.

FACT FILE

Scientific name *Erica tetralix*
Type Heather family
Height Up to 70 cm
Flowers July to September
Fruit Small, downy, dark-brown capsules

Egg-shaped flower

Pink flowers droop

Flower is 6 mm long

Many flowers in each cluster

Narrow, sticky leaves, with hairs

Small leaves

Whorls of four leaves arranged around the stem

DEPTFORD PINK

The colour of this flower's petals is often described as cerise, and its stem is greyish. Deptford pinks are biennial, which means that their life cycle takes two years. This plant produces up to 400 seeds at the end of the summer. A round clump, or rosette, of leaves grows the following year, and flowers bloom the year after that.

ACTUAL SIZE

Sweet Williams are related to Deptford pinks, and are popular in gardens. Their flowers are larger than those of Deptford pinks, and grow in a range of colours.

FACT FILE

Scientific name
Dianthus armeria

Type Pink family

Height Up to 60 cm

Flowers June to August

Fruit Small capsules

Flowers grow at top of stems

Five petals

Thin leaves, with hairs

Straight, slender stem

FOXGLOVE

This flower is easy to spot, with its tall spikes that are covered in up to 80 pink flowers. The plant gets its name from the tube-shaped flowers, which are said to resemble little gloves for a fox. The large, pale-green leaves are soft on top and woolly underneath.

As bees crawl into a foxglove flower, they get covered in pollen. They transfer pollen to other flowers. In doing so they fertilize the eggs, which then grow into seeds.

FACT FILE

Scientific name
Digitalis purpurea

Type Figwort family

Height 40–150 cm

Flowers June to August

Fruit Green capsules

Pink-purple flowers

Raceme (flower spike) with 20 to 80 flowers on it

Seed case

Flower is 4 cm long

Inside the flower there is a white part, purple spots and hairs

Woolly stem and leaves

GREAT WILLOWHERB

Willowherbs are unusually tall wildflowers, so it is easy to find them in damp places throughout Britain, except the far northwest, where they rarely grow. They can come from seeds, but they also spread out by fattened roots, called rhizomes, in the soil. This can lead to a large, colourful clump forming in one spot.

ACTUAL SIZE

These flowers are called codlins-and-cream because they are pink and white. Codlins were rosy apples that were boiled in milk and served with cream.

FACT FILE

Scientific name
Epilobium hirsutum

Type Willowherb family

Height Up to 200 cm

Flowers July and August

Fruit Soft pods contain airborne seeds

Flowerless stalk

Rosy-pink petals attract bees and hoverflies

Flower is 25 mm across

Creamy-white stigma

Long, narrow, pointed leaves

Woolly stems and leaves

HEATHER

You can find heather in both damp and dry places. It grows into bushes with many branches and each bush can reach 100 cm tall and 100 cm wide. Heather keeps its leaves over winter, and its flowers, which are sometimes white, can last until autumn. This species is known as 'common heather' or 'ling'.

ACTUAL SIZE

Heather was once used as bedding for animals and bound together to make rope, brooms and thatch for roofs.

FACT FILE

Scientific name
Calluna vulgaris

Type Heather family

Height 50–100 cm

Flowers July to September

Fruit Capsules

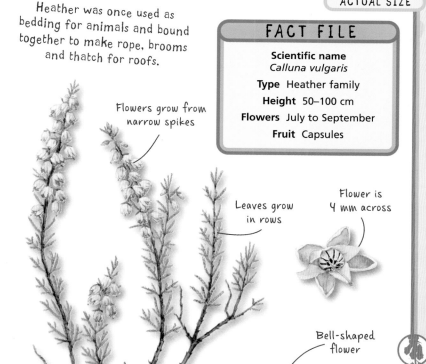

Flowers grow from narrow spikes

Leaves grow in rows

Flower is 4 mm across

Bell-shaped flower

Woody stem

HERB-ROBERT

Herb-Robert is a survivor. It can live in sun or shade, and can cope with mild winter weather, unlike many other wildflowers that die down after summer. As Herb-Robert is not fussy about the type of soil it lives in, it is common throughout Britain.

Herb-Robert turns red in autumn. Although it is very pretty, this plant can quickly take over an area, killing off weaker plants that cannot reach the light.

ACTUAL SIZE

FACT FILE

Scientific name
Geranium robertianum

Type Crane's-bill family

Height 10–50 cm

Flowers April to October

Fruit Long and hairy

Five petals on a flower, can be pink or white

Flower is 12 mm across

Seed case

Feathery leaves

Red stems, hairy and oily

INDIAN BALSAM

This plant was introduced to Britain in 1839, having been brought from the Himalayan mountain region. It is one of the tallest wildflowers, and is seen all over Britain, especially in England and Wales. In some places in the UK, it is outcompeting native plants and is treated as an invasive weed.

ACTUAL SIZE

In some places, Indian balsam is called 'bee-bums', because when a bee is exploring inside the flower, feeding on nectar, all you can see is its tail end!

FACT FILE

Scientific name
Impatiens glandulifera

Type Balsam family

Height 100–200 cm

Flowers July to October

Fruit Explosive seed pods

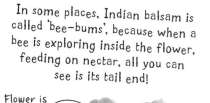

Flower is
3 cm across

Orchid-like
flowers

Explosive
seed pod

Slender leaves
with toothed
edges

Reddish
stems

PURPLE-LOOSESTRIFE

Found growing close together in wet places, purple-loosestrife has magenta-pink flower spikes standing tall above the green leaves. These plants are perennial, which means they can live for more than two years before dying down, and the flowers last for the whole summer.

ACTUAL SIZE

Clumps of purple-loosestrife attract many types of wildlife, including bumblebees, honeybees, brimstone butterflies and elephant hawk-moths.

FACT FILE

Scientific name
Lythrum salicaria

Type Loosestrife family

Height Up to 200 cm

Flowers June to August

Fruit Capsule containing tiny seeds

Petals are red-pink

Six petals

Flower is 15 mm across

Flowers grow on upright stalks

Long, slender leaves grow in pairs, opposite each other

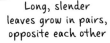

RED CAMPION

The flowers of red campion are mostly pink rather than red. There are five petals on each flowerhead, but it can look as if there are more when the petals are very deeply lobed. The flowers are visited by bumblebees, butterflies and moths, which feed on the sweet nectar.

ACTUAL SIZE

Red campion blooms as bluebells are finishing. Woodlands with wood anemones, bluebells and red campion go through shades of white, blue and pink from spring to autumn.

FACT FILE

Scientific name
Silene dioica
Type Pink family
Height Up to 100 cm
Flowers March to October
Fruit Round, dry capsule

Pink petals, occasionally with red tips

Flower is up to 25 mm across

Seed capsule

Long, hairy stems, slightly sticky

Oval, hairy leaves in pairs

THRIFT

This flower has candyfloss flowerheads growing above a dense mat of leaves. It is an unusual plant that can grow in very dry places, especially at the coast. The clump of leaves makes a safe home for beetles and other insects, and bees visit the pink flowers. When many clumps grow together, they create a cushion of soft leaves.

ACTUAL SIZE

According to folklore, if you have thrift in your garden you will never be poor. Named after the practice of taking care of your money, it was depicted on the back of an old English coin.

FACT FILE

Scientific name
Armeria maritima
Type Thrift family
Height Up to 20 cm
Flowers April to October
Fruit Capsules

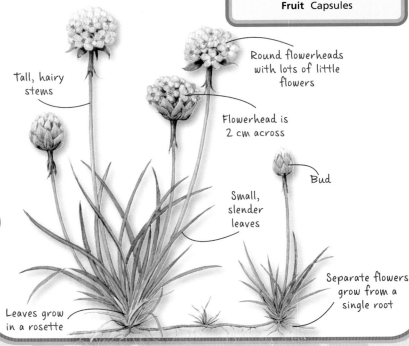

Tall, hairy stems

Round flowerheads with lots of little flowers

Flowerhead is 2 cm across

Small, slender leaves

Bud

Separate flowers grow from a single root

Leaves grow in a rosette

MARSH CINQUEFOIL

The deep pink or red flowers of the marsh cinquefoil are unlike any other flower. They are star shaped, and grow at the top of upright magenta-coloured stems. There are five sepals and smaller purple petals form a layer on top of them. Other cinquefoils, which grow in dry places, have yellow flowers and are not star shaped.

ACTUAL SIZE

Although the flower of this plant is very distinctive, you can still recognize it when it is not in bloom by its large, toothed leaves, which are mostly divided into five leaflets.

FACT FILE

Scientific name
Potentilla palustris

Type Rose family

Height 20–50 cm

Flowers June and July

Fruit Dry, small and papery

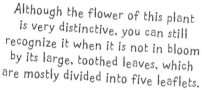

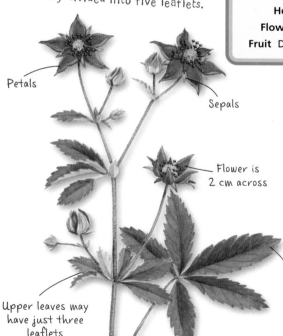

Petals

Sepals

Flower is 2 cm across

Upper leaves may have just three leaflets

Lowest leaves may have five leaflets

PHEASANT'S EYE

A type of buttercup, pheasant's eye has five to eight glossy scarlet petals and feathery leaves. By August the flowers are dying down to be replaced by large seed cases. When the seeds fall to the ground they may rest there – they are described as 'dormant' – until the following spring, or even several years later.

ACTUAL SIZE

This flower is rare, as each plant only produces a few heavy seeds that are not easily transported to new areas. It has also been killed off in many areas by the use of chemicals.

FACT FILE

Scientific name
Adonis annua

Type Buttercup family

Height Up to 40 cm

Flowers June to August

Fruit Large and wrinkled

Black centre

Red petals, black at the base

Flower is 3 cm across

Large seed case

Feathery, delicate leaves

POPPY

The scarlet, papery petals of the poppy **are often black at the base.** A flower grows at the top of each long, hairy stalk. The leaves are distinctive, with their feathery appearance and toothed edges.

Poppies are common in farmers' fields because they grow particularly well on soil that has been disturbed, and they can flower and seed themselves before the farmer's crop is harvested.

ACTUAL SIZE

FACT FILE

Scientific name
Papaver rhoeas
Type Poppy family
Height 40–80 cm
Flowers June to August
Fruit Round capsule

Four petals

Flower is 7 cm across

Seed head droops

Tough seed case

Hairy stalks

Long slender leaves, divided to give a feathery appearance

31

SCARLET PIMPERNEL

It is easy to overlook the tiny red flowers
of the scarlet pimpernel. These plants are
small and grow low to the ground, with
the stems sprawling out along the soil.
Purple hairs inside the flower attract many
insects in summer. Scarlet pimpernels are
common throughout Britain, but in
Scotland are mostly found near the coast.

ACTUAL SIZE

The petals of scarlet pimpernel close
when air pressure drops — a sign
that rain might be due. It can also
be used to tell the time, as petals
open in the morning and close
mid-afternoon.

FACT FILE

Scientific name
Anagallis arvensis
Type Primrose family
Height Up to 20 cm
Flowers May to September
Fruit Tiny brown capsules

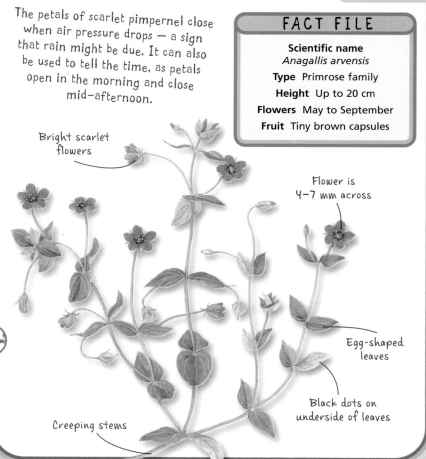

Bright scarlet
flowers

Flower is
4–7 mm across

Egg-shaped
leaves

Black dots on
underside of leaves

Creeping stems

BLUEBELL

These plants normally bear blue flowers, but there are violet, pink and white ones, too. Flower spikes grow from a clump of deep-green leaves. Each spike bears 4–16 bell-shaped flowers in clusters. Bluebells were once common, but many bluebell woods have been damaged by people picking the flowers and digging up the bulbs.

ACTUAL SIZE

Beautiful bluebells carpet woodland floors in spring, creating a stunning sight.

FACT FILE

Scientific name
Hyacinthoides non-scripta
Type Lily family
Height 10–40 cm
Flowers April to June
Fruit Capsules

Flower is 15 mm long

As the flowers open they droop, like bells

Flower spikes (racemes) are upright when in bud

Papery seed case

Strong, long and glossy leaves

BROOKLIME

Acreeping plant, brooklime produces stems that grow along the ground. Roots grow from these stems at places called nodes. The flowering stems grow upright and produce star-shaped blooms throughout the summer. The petals are usually blue, but pink ones also grow and there is a white 'eye' in the centre of each bloom.

ACTUAL SIZE

Brooklime grows in wet ground and in water. Its leaves and stems provide shelter for small pond-living animals such as insects and tadpoles.

FACT FILE

Scientific name
Veronica beccabunga

Type Water plant of the Speedwell family

Height Up to 30 cm

Flowers May to September

Fruit Round, flat capsules

Small, blue flowers

Four petals

Oval, fleshy leaves

Flower is 3 cm across

Creeping stems

Root

BUGLE

This plant forms dense mats of green leaves, covering the ground. Flower stems grow upwards and bear clusters of many small, purple flowers. Occasionally, the flowers are pink or white. Bugle leaves are unusual because they have a dark green background colour, with a purple sheen. Butterflies often flitter around this plant and feed on it.

ACTUAL SIZE

In some places bugle is called carpenter's herb, because it was once used to stop bleeding and people often grew it in their gardens for that purpose.

FACT FILE

Scientific name
Ajuga reptans
Type Dead-nettle family
Height Up to 20 cm
Flowers April to June
Fruit Nutlets

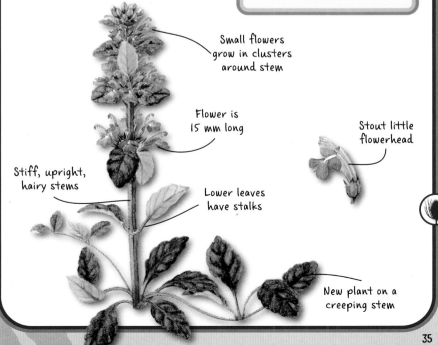

Small flowers grow in clusters around stem

Flower is 15 mm long

Stout little flowerhead

Stiff, upright, hairy stems

Lower leaves have stalks

New plant on a creeping stem

BUTTERWORT

These violet flowers attract bees to pollinate them. A sticky leaf attracts flies and other small insects, holding them like glue and stopping them from breathing. The leaves then curl around the bugs and produce chemicals that start to dissolve their bodies. This releases nutrients that help the plant to grow.

ACTUAL SIZE

Flowers grow from single stems, which emerge out of a single rosette of leaves at ground level.

FACT FILE

Scientific name
Pinguicula vulgaris
Type Bladderwort family
Height Up to 15 cm
Flowers May to August
Fruit Tough, oval-shaped capsule

Funnel-shaped flower

Flower is 12 mm across

White at base

Yellow-green, sticky leaves

Rosette of leaves at base of plant

COLUMBINE

The flowers of columbine grow on tall stems. The central part of the flower is made up of five petals, and a rosette of coloured leaves surrounds them, to create a drooping, stunning bloom. Wild columbines are deep blue to purple in colour and have a fragrance.

ACTUAL SIZE

Columbine is poisonous but it was once used to treat digestive problems, and as a painkiller. It was also thought that carrying a posy of columbine would make people fall in love.

FACT FILE

Scientific name
Aquilegia vulgaris
Type Buttercup family
Height Up to 100 cm
Flowers May to August
Fruit Small and dry but with many seeds

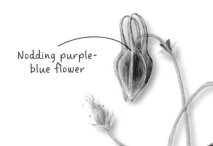

Nodding purple-blue flower

Flower is 35 mm long

Grey-green leaves, divided

Leafless stem

Leaves grow as a clump at the ground

CORNFLOWER

Cornflower blooms are such a brilliant blue that they have given their name to a shade of the colour. Each bloom is actually a collection of tiny flowers, called florets. The outer florets are blue to purple, and the inner florets are slightly redder. Cornflowers were once common in farmers' fields, but are now a rare sight.

ACTUAL SIZE

Cornflowers were used in herbal medicine to treat eye problems, and young men in love often wore them in their buttonholes.

FACT FILE

Scientific name
Centaurea cyanus

Type Daisy family

Height 40–90 cm

Flowers June to August

Fruit Small

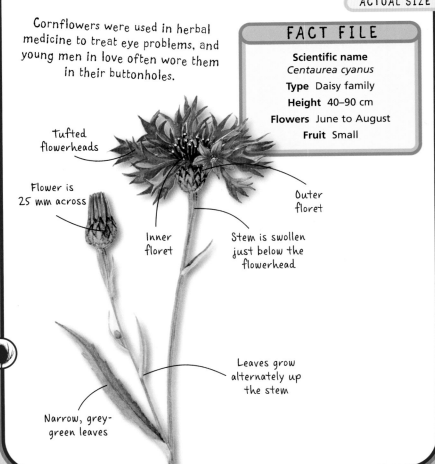

Tufted flowerheads

Flower is 25 mm across

Inner floret

Outer floret

Stem is swollen just below the flowerhead

Leaves grow alternately up the stem

Narrow, grey-green leaves

DEVIL'S-BIT SCABIOUS

The round bloom of a Devil's-bit scabious is not one flower, but many little florets all clustered together. The petals are usually purple-blue, but are sometimes pinkish. The tiny anthers in each flower poke out above the petals. Bumblebees are drawn to the flowers because they prefer purple blooms to those of any other colour.

ACTUAL SIZE

Insects are attracted to these flowers because they feed on the sugary nectar that the flowers produce. In return, the insects pollinate the plants.

FACT FILE

Scientific name
Succisa pratensis

Type Teasel family

Height 10–75 cm

Flowers June to September

Fruit Dry and papery

Flower is 2 cm across

Domed flowerhead

Stems may be hairy

Upright stem

Leaves mostly grow near bottom of stem

HAREBELL

The flowers of the harebell are delicate and swing when a breeze catches them. Each stem may bear just one flower, or several growing on a spike. The leaves grow long and thin near the flowers, but round when they are near the base. At ground level, creeping stems become thick and store food over winter for the plant.

Harebells can live from year to year because they grow rhizomes. In autumn, the plants die down but the rhizomes are safe in the ground, and produce new stems in spring.

FACT FILE

Scientific name
Campanula rotundifolia

Type Harebell family

Height 10–40 cm

Flowers July to October

Fruit Dry capsules

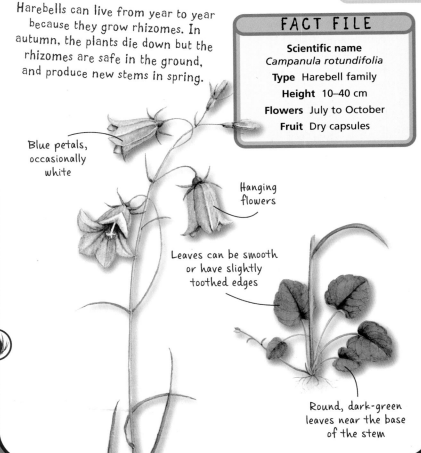

Blue petals, occasionally white

Hanging flowers

Leaves can be smooth or have slightly toothed edges

Round, dark-green leaves near the base of the stem

MARSH VIOLET

Violets look like pansies, but are a little smaller. Marsh violet flowers are pale lilac or violet in colour and the lower petal has deep purple veins. After the flower dies the petals fall off, but the five sepals stay attached to the stalk and the growing seed capsule. The caterpillars of fritillary butterflies use this as a food plant.

ACTUAL SIZE

Wild pansies are also part of the violet family and they grow in dry grasslands and gardens. Their flowers can be violet, yellow or a combination of the two.

FACT FILE

Scientific name
Viola palustris

Type Violet family

Height 5–20 cm

Flowers April to July

Fruit Egg-shaped

Four upright petals

Stalks droop at the top

Long stalks

Flower is 12 mm across

Lower petal is large and lobed

Leaves are kidney shaped or round

MEADOW CRANE'S BILL

The purple-blue flowers of the meadow crane's bill grow tall above the surface of a clump of dark-green leaves, providing a summer splash of colour. These flowers grow all over Britain but look similar to wood crane's bill, which is paler in colour, but is only found in the north of England and Scotland.

ACTUAL SIZE

Crane's bills are also called geraniums. They can survive from year to year, and grow in bigger and bigger mounds. Most geraniums are blue, violet, purple or pink.

FACT FILE

Scientific name
Geranium pratense
Type Crane's bill family
Height 20–80 cm
Flowers June to September
Fruit Small but with a long 'beak'

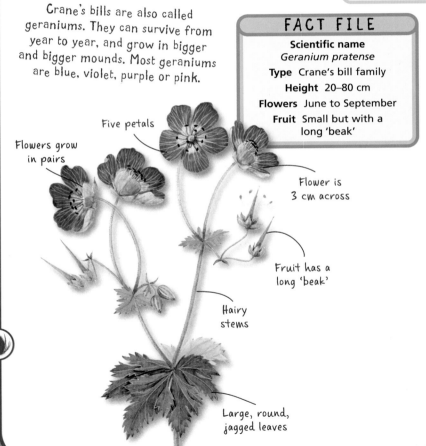

Five petals

Flowers grow in pairs

Flower is 3 cm across

Fruit has a long 'beak'

Hairy stems

Large, round, jagged leaves

SEA PEA

Pretty sea pea plants provide colour to dry areas of shingle beaches. Their delicate leaves and tendrils spread out in clumps up to 2 m wide. Sea peas rarely flower before their third summer. The pea-like seeds are carried by seawater to new areas, and can survive for up to five years before they start to grow into new plants.

ACTUAL SIZE

The seeds are still able to germinate if they've been in water for up to five years.

FACT FILE

Scientific name
Lathyrus japonicus
Type Pea family
Size Up to 20 cm
Flowers From May to August
Fruit Pods containing seeds

Flowers grow in a cluster of up to nine flowers

Tendrils

Seed pod contains up to eight seeds

Oval leaves arranged along stalks

Blue-green leaves

43

TEASEL

Teasel plants produce flowers only in their second year. In the first year, the plant grows a large rosette of leaves at ground level. In the second year, a large stem grows from the rosette to hold the flowerhead. The rosette then dies back and paired prickly leaves grow on the flower stem.

SCALE

Teasels are especially popular with goldfinches. These bold, noisy, colourful birds flock to the dry heads to feast on the seeds inside.

FACT FILE

Scientific name
Dipsacus fullonum

Type Teasel family

Height Up to 200 cm

Flowers July and August

Fruit Dry flowerheads hold many dry fruits

Flower is 7 cm long

Prickly leaves and flower stem

Large flowerhead, about 7 cm long, with purple flowers

Leaves have no stalks and grow in pairs

TUFTED VETCH

Like other members of the pea family, tufted vetch has many oval leaflets that are paired on one stalk. Curling tendrils grow from the end of some leaflets. They help pea plants to climb and clamber high, catching the sun and blocking the light from other plants. The blue-purple flowers grow in clusters where leaflets connect to the stem.

ACTUAL SIZE

Tufted vetch is also known as cow vetch because it can be fed to cattle. It grows in wild woodlands where deer may roam. Like other pea plants, it adds goodness to the soil.

FACT FILE

Scientific name
Vicia cracca

Type Pea family

Height 30–200 cm

Flowers June to August

Fruit Bright-green pods

Clusters of flowers on a one-sided spike

Blue-purple flower

Flower is one cm long

Long, hairy pods

Branched tendril

Up to 12 pairs of leaflets on one stalk

COWSLIP

These flowers were once widespread, but have become less common in recent years. Cowslips have rosettes of large, wrinkled leaves at the base and clusters of yellow flowers that are held high on tall stems. Today, hedgerows and meadows are often left uncut until autumn, so flowers like these have a better chance of surviving.

ACTUAL SIZE

Cowslips have long been used in traditional medicine to treat coughs and headaches. They can also be made into wine, or used to add flavour and colour to recipes.

FACT FILE

Scientific name
Primula veris
Type Primrose family
Height 10–30 cm
Flowers April and May
Fruit Capsules

Yellow flowers in a cluster

Tall stem

Tubular shaped sepals

Flower is 12 mm across

Each leaf about 12 cm long

Thick, wrinkly leaves in a rosette

DANDELION

One of the most common flowering plants, dandelions are found in gardens, parks and woodlands. They are often considered to be weeds, but their bright-yellow flowers are a favourite of many pollinating insects. Other types of wildlife, such as rabbits, enjoy eating both flowers and leaves. The plants grow in a rosette shape, with the leaves and flower stem coming out of a central point, just above the tap root.

SCALE

Dandelions get their name from the old French name for the plant, 'dent de lion'. This means 'tooth of the lion' because the leaf edges look like a row of sharp teeth.

FACT FILE

Scientific name
Taraxacum officinale

Type Asteraceae family

Height 5–74 cm

Flowers March to October

Fruit Tiny seeds with fluffy hairs

Bright-yellow flowers

Dandelion seeds are fluffy and lightweight

Hollow, fleshy flower stalk with white sap inside

Rosette of bracts around central stem

Long stalk

Lobed leaves

FLAX-LEAVED ST JOHN'S WORT

This plant has golden yellow flowers, each with five petals. After the flowers die down the seed capsules split, releasing up to 250 tiny seeds that are carried by the wind. This plant is very rare in Britain, and is only found in parts of North Wales and on Dartmoor in southwest England, and a few other scattered locations.

ACTUAL SIZE

More common St John's wort plants are similar to the flax-leaved type, but they mostly have more obvious anthers and can grow to a height of one metre.

FACT FILE

Scientific name
Hypericum linarifolium
Type St John's wort family
Height Up to 30 cm
Flowers June and July
Fruit Brown capsule

Yellow or orange-yellow petals

Long, thin stamens

Flower is 8–12 mm across

Slender, straight leaves

Leaf up to 30 mm long

LESSER CELANDINE

Found in woodlands and other natural habitats, lesser celandine grows as a patch of rosettes on the ground, topped by bright-yellow flowers. However, it dies back once flowering has finished. The flowers contain between eight and 12 little petals, which only open when the sun is shining.

ACTUAL SIZE

Lesser celandine is one of the first wildflowers to bloom. It provides food for insects, especially hungry bumblebees that have just come out of hibernation.

FACT FILE

Scientific name
Ranunculus ficaria

Type Buttercup family

Height 2–20 cm

Flowers March to May

Fruit Rounded seed heads

Flower is 2–3 cm across

Eight petals around yellow stamens

Leaves are green and glossy

Heart-shaped leaves

MARSH MARIGOLD

This plant is tough and can survive in shady or sunny places, but it prefers damp soil. Marsh marigolds can form large clumps of deep-green, shiny leaves, topped by bright, golden flowers. They used to be common, but many of their marsh and bog habitats have disappeared.

ACTUAL SIZE

These brightly coloured flowers were sometimes scattered over doorsteps in May. They were also used to remove warts and cure colds.

FACT FILE

Scientific name
Caltha palustris

Type Buttercup family

Height 20–30 cm

Flowers March to July

Fruit Capsules

Five yellow sepals

Flower is 25 mm across

Kidney-shaped leaf

Strong, upright stem

PRIMROSE

The yellow petals of the primrose are as pale as butter, but they turn orange near their bases. Primrose's Latin name – *Primula* – comes from the Latin for 'first little one' and 'primrose' means 'first rose'. This is one of the early spring flowering plants that bloom when there are few other flowers around.

ACTUAL SIZE

The base of each primrose petal is an orange-yellow, giving a golden centre to each flower. Many flowers grow, topping slender stalks that emerge from a central rosette of leaves.

FACT FILE

Scientific name
Primula vulgaris

Type Primrose family

Height 10–30 cm

Flowers March to June

Fruit Capsules

Flower is 25 mm across

Five petals, lobed

Rosette of leaves

Oval, crinkly leaves

SILVERWEED

This is a creeping plant that spreads out on bare soils. The feathery leaves are divided up into many pairs of leaflets that are covered in fine, silvery hairs. Long creeping stems, called stolons, grow on the ground beneath the leaves and flowers. Silverweed has been used in herbal remedies, and its roots were used to make tea.

ACTUAL SIZE

Silverweed appears in many old stories and folklore. It was regarded as a useful plant, and its leaves were even put in shoes to keep feet dry!

FACT FILE

Scientific name
Potentilla anserina

Type Rose family

Height 5–20 cm

Flowers May to August

Fruit Dry and papery

Five petals

Silvery hairs on leaves

Flower is 15 mm across

Long, creeping stem

Up to 12 leaflets on a leaf

SUNFLOWER

These tall flowering plants grow as a single stem with a huge flowerhead that can measure up to 30 cm across. A sunflower plant may reach 3 m in height. They are also grown by farmers as crops. The seeds can be eaten as a snack or added to cooking, but more importantly, they can be used to produce sunflower oil. This oil is used for cooking and as a fuel for cars.

SCALE

Sunflowers are easy plants to grow. A single seed in a pot of compost will germinate in just a couple of weeks, if it is watered regularly and kept in a light place.

FACT FILE

Scientific name *Helianthus*

Type Daisy family

Height Up to 3 m

Flowers Mid to late summer

Fruit Medium-sized seeds, after flowering

Yellow petals

Centre of flowerhead is packed with hundreds of seeds

Large flowerhead, 30 cm wide

Very tall stem

Thick, hollow stem

Large leaves

YELLOW IRIS

Irises grow in wet places, and may even have their roots in water. They can spread by means of seeds, but also spread by rhizomes, which are swollen roots that produce buds in spring. When they spread by rhizomes, irises can quickly grow into large clumps and create a perfect habitat for pond wildlife.

SCALE

Ducks, fish and insects can hide among iris plants. Yellow irises remove dirt from water, and are used in sewage farms.

FACT FILE

Scientific name
Iris pseudocorus
Type Iris family
Height Up to 1 m
Flowers June to August
Fruit Three-sided and long

Long, slender anthers

Flower is 9 cm across

Large green sepals protect flower bud

Large flowers with floppy petals

Long, slender leaves may survive mild winters

YELLOW RATTLE

This plant steals nutrients from its neighbouring plants. It stops grass from growing, which helps other types of wild plant to survive in meadows. At the end of summer the seed capsules ripen and seeds inside become loose. When the capsule is shaken, the seeds rattle around, which is how the plant got its name.

ACTUAL SIZE

The stems of yellow rattle have unusual black marks on them, which helps to identify this meadow wildflower. The yellow flowers are small, and protected by green bracts.

FACT FILE

Scientific name
Rhinanthus minor
Type Figwort family
Height 20–40 cm
Flowers June to September
Fruit Dry capsules with seeds that rattle

Flower is up to 20 mm long

Small flower has hooded petal above and lipped petal below

Stiff, upright stem

Green bracts (scale-like leaves)

Leaves are triangular in shape, ribbed and toothed

GLOSSARY

Annual A plant that takes one year to complete its life cycle.

Berry A small, soft fruit with small seeds.

Biennial A plant that takes two years to complete its life cycle.

Bloom When the flowers open.

Bract A scale-like leaf that grows at the bottom of some flower stalks.

Bud The flowerhead before it opens.

Bulb A swollen part of the plant that grows underground, or at ground level. It contains the beginnings of the next year's stems and leaves.

Floret A small flower that is part of a bigger flowerhead.

Habitat The place where a plant lives.

Leaflet A leaf can have several parts that look like little leaves, called leaflets.

Life cycle The stages that a plant goes through during its life.

Nectar The sweet liquid made by some flowers.

Perennial A plant that lives for more than two years.

Petal The coloured parts of the flowerhead.

Pollen A powder made by flowers. It is carried to other flowers so they can produce new seeds.

Raceme A hanging group of flowers.

Rhizome A thickened stem that grows underground or at ground level.

Rosette The way leaves are arranged around a stem at ground level.

Season One of the periods that a year is divided into, such as spring, summer, autumn and winter.

Seed A small fruit produced by a plant. New plants grow from seeds.

Sepal One of the small leaves under the flower.

Spadix A flower spike.

Spathe A thick leaf that protects the growing flower.

Stalk The long, narrow part of a plant that supports the leaves, flowers and fruit, and carries water and nutrients up them.

Stamen The male part of a flower that makes pollen.

Stem The long, thin part of a plant, from which the leaves and flowers grow.

Stigma One of the female parts of a flower.

Style One of the female parts of a flower.

Tendril A thin growth that wraps itself around things.

Weed A wild plant that grows where it is not wanted.

Good Luck, Bad Luck

Sam Carter

Illustrated by
Dan Chernett

LONDON·SYDNEY

For the new readers at Dorrington School – be lucky! DS

First published in 2009
by Franklin Watts

Text © Deborah Smith 2009
Illustrations © Dan Chernett 2009
Cover design by Peter Scoulding

Franklin Watts
338 Euston Road
London NW1 3BH

Franklin Watts Australia
Level 17/207 Kent Street
Sydney, NSW 2000

A CIP catalogue record for this book
is available from the British Library.

ISBN: 978 0 7496 9042 7

1 3 5 7 9 10 8 6 4 2

Printed in Great Britain by J F Print Ltd., Sparkford

Franklin Watts is a division of Hachette Children's Books,
an Hachette UK company.
www.hachette.co.uk

Harvey, Sam, Amber, Ravi, Jade and Lewis are: THE CREW

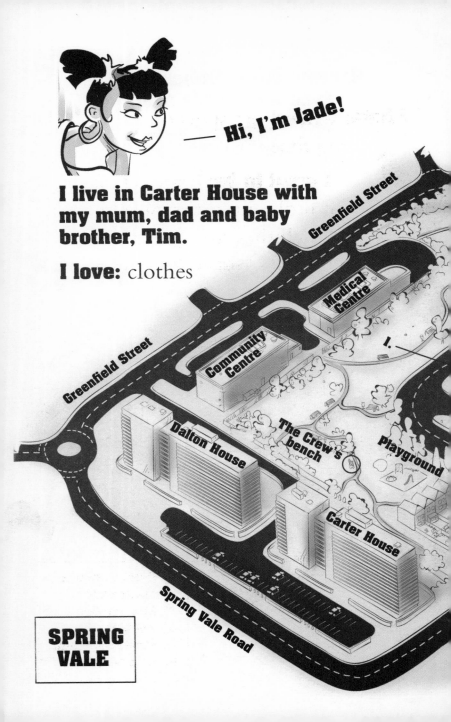

I hate: when I get spots on my face

I want to be: a model, or a make-up artist, or own a clothes store

Best word: fashion

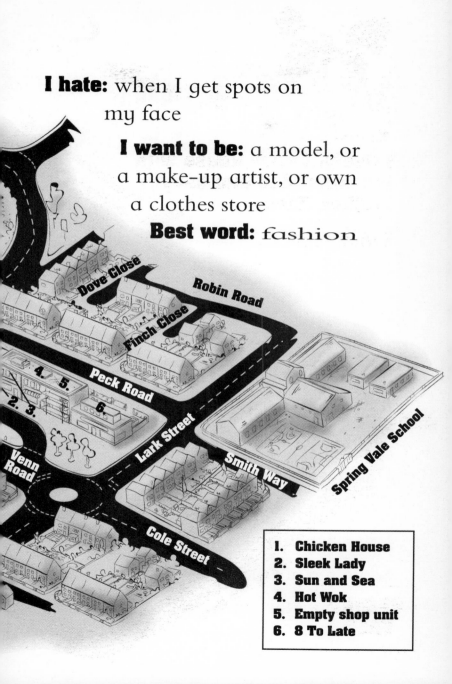

1. **Chicken House**
2. **Sleek Lady**
3. **Sun and Sea**
4. **Hot Wok**
5. **Empty shop unit**
6. **8 To Late**

Chapter One

It's Saturday morning.

Mum is out at the shops.

Dad has gone to work at Hot Wok.

I can stay in bed as long as I want.

Later, I can hang out with the Crew.

Saturdays are the best!

I turn over, for just one more snooze...

Then – ARGGHH!

A great lump lands on me.

It's Ming, our big fat cat.

I leap out of bed.

"MING!" I yell. "That was mean!"

9

I'm up now and WIDE AWAKE.

I've got loads of time until I meet the Crew.

I wash, get dressed and have some toast and jam.

I drink all of the banana milk
(sorry Mum!).

Then I go and check my e-mail.

What's this one?

OPEN ME NOW – TO STOP BAD LUCK!

I open it – quickly!

It says…

HELLO.

SEND THIS E-MAIL ON TO TEN PEOPLE.

THIS MUST BE DONE IN ONE HOUR.

IF NOT, YOU WILL HAVE BAD LUCK ALL DAY.

Oh no! That's nasty!

I don't want bad luck all day.

So I start to send the e-mail on.

First I send it to the Crew – easy.

Amber

Harvey

Sam

Ravi

Lewis – that's five.

Then I send it to Dad – six.

My cousin Poppy – seven.

Who else? I can't think!

Oh, my little cousin Bella – that's eight, and Uncle Nic – nine.

One more person…

But then the doorbell rings, so I go to see who it is.

Gran is at the door.

She holds up her sewing bag.

"Your new top, Jade," she says.
"Come and try!"

Gran makes me lots of stuff.

She's the best at sewing.

"Great! OK, Gran," I say. "But first,
I just need to send—"

Gran shakes her head. "Try now!"
she says.

The top is just what I wanted.

"I love it, Gran!" I tell her.

Gran smiles as she pins the sleeves.

"That's good!" she says.

Then she starts to pin the hem.

I look back at the computer.

I look at the clock. The hour is nearly up.

"Keep still, Jade!" Gran says. "You are like a slippery eel!"

19

At last! Gran puts her pins away.

"I must go to Hot Wok now,"
she says. "I'll finish your top later."

I give her a kiss.

"Thanks, Gran," I say. "You're
the best."

Then I rush over to the computer.

But the hour was up long ago.

I'd better watch out.

I'm in for bad luck!

Chapter Two

Time to meet the Crew.

On the way, I call in at Hot Wok.

Dad is at the counter.

"Want to take some fortune cookies?"
he asks.

I grin. "Yes please!" I say.

He gives me a large bag.

No bad luck so far…

23

The rest of the Crew are chilling at our bench.

I wave and walk over there.

"Hey, Jade!" they all say.

"You've got fortune cookies!" Lewis yells.

I open the bag and we all take one.

"I got that bad luck e-mail you sent,"
Ravi tells me.

"Did you send it on?" I ask him.

"Nah!" he says.

"But what about the bad luck thing?"
I ask.

The Crew just shake their heads.

"It's just mumbo jumbo, Jade!"
Sam says.

"Yeah, it's rubbish," Amber says.

But I'm not so sure…

Harvey snaps open his cookie.

He takes out the paper and reads it.

"Let your heart open like a flower…"

We all fall about laughing.

"A pretty little flower, Harvey!"
Amber teases.

Harvey folds his arms, in a sulk.

"Fortune cookies are mumbo jumbo
too!" he says.

I hold the cookie bag out to him.

"Try again," I tell him.

Harvey pulls out a cookie and
opens it.

"Let the world hear you…"
he reads.

Then he grins. "Yeah – I'm gonna
be in a famous band!"

Chapter Three

When all the cookies have been eaten, we go for a walk.

I think about the bad luck e-mail.

"We need to take care," I say.

The others roll their eyes at me.

But I still worry.

We see a man painting a wall.

He's at the top of a tall ladder.

Lewis and Ravi go to walk under it.

"Don't do that!" I yell. "It's bad luck!"

"Why?" Lewis asks.

But I'm not sure why.

"Paint will splash down on you, stupid!" Amber tells him.

Thanks, Amber!

33

Lewis still walks under the ladder.

"Look – no paint!" he calls.

He turns round and round to show us.

Amber and me shrug.

Then Harvey walks under the ladder, too.

"Hey, what's that?" he asks.

Lewis bends down and picks it up.

"Look!" he says.

It's a £5 note.

"Boy!" Harvey yells. "That's GOOD luck, man!"

We all go to 8 To Late to spend the money.

This is what we get:

Six bags of crisps — one each.

Two big bags of sweets — to share.

One big bottle of cola — to share.

Then we take it all back to our bench.

We eat our crisps first and pass the cola round.

Then Sam spits out a big crisp.

"Urgh! Sam!" yells Amber. "That's nasty!"

"Sorry," Sam says. "But it's not a crisp, it's—"

"A £20 note!" says Ravi. "You have a lucky bag with a cash prize!"

We all cheer.

So much for bad luck today!

Chapter Four

"Jade, get up!" Mum calls next morning. "Gran's here."

I go and say hello in my PJs.

Gran holds out my new top – it's finished!

I give her a big hug.

"I'm gonna try it on!" I tell her.

I come back out to show them all.

Gran nods and smiles.

"You look like me when I was a girl!" she says.

41

"Can I wear it today?" I ask.

Mum frowns. "Let's keep it for best, Jade," she says.

"But I SO want to wear it now!" I tell her.

"Well, if Gran says OK…" Mum says with a smile.

We all look at Gran.

She nods.

Result!

Soon after, I'm washed and dressed.

I go to check my e-mail again.

There's a new message.

OPEN ME NOW – TO BRING GOOD LUCK!

Do I want good luck? Yes, please!

I open the e-mail.

It says…

HELLO, JADE

SEND THIS E-MAIL ON TO TEN PEOPLE.

THIS MUST BE DONE IN ONE HOUR.

THEN YOU WILL HAVE GOOD LUCK ALL DAY!

So this time I send the e-mail on.

Goodbye bad luck day.

Hello good luck day!

Chapter Five

It's time to meet the Crew.

I stop off at Hot Wok.

"Do you want cookies today, Jade?" Dad asks me.

"No thanks, Dad," I tell him. "We're gonna buy crisps."

Me and the Crew, we have a cheeky plan…

Sam brings his £20 note.

"So, we spend it all on more crisps," he says. "Agreed?"

"Agreed," we say.

"Then we'll find more lucky bags – and be rich!" Lewis yells.

"Sshhh, Lewis!" we all say. "It's our secret."

But I'm sure I will find a lucky bag – maybe more than one.

I've got good luck all day!

We head over to 8 To Late.

Each packet of crisps is 50p.

With the £20 we buy 40 bags of crisps.

Ravi's uncle, who owns the shop, looks shocked.

"You must really like crisps!" he says.

"Oh, yes, Uncle, we do," Ravi tells him.

We try to hide our grins.

Sam hands over the money.

Then we all hurry out.

We sit in a ring on the grass.

Sam tips all the crisp bags into the middle.

"I'll go first," he says.

He picks up a bag and opens it.

But there's no £20.

I can't wait for my turn.

I'm sure I'll get a lucky bag!

"Here goes!" I say.

Is there £20 in it?

NO!

We keep opening the bags.

None of them have money in.

Sam opens the last bag – it's just crisps.

"None of them was a lucky bag!"
he says.

"I feel sick!" moans Lewis.

"That's coz you ate too many crisps!"
Amber snaps.

"I have beef breath! Smell?" says
Harvey.

"Yuck! NO!" I say.

Then my phone rings. It's Gran.

"Very busy at Hot Wok, Jade – come
and wash up, please!"

What? So much for a good luck day!

57

I say bye to the Crew.

Then I walk over to Hot Wok.

On the way, I spot a four leaf clover in the grass.

At last! A four leaf clover is lucky!

I bend down to pick it up and RIIIPP!

The sleeve of my new top comes apart.

Then I see dog poo on my boot.

Lucky? Huh!

After a HUGE pile of washing up,
I go home.

Just before bed, I check my e-mail.

There's a new one…

OPEN ME NOW – TO HAVE A GOOD LUCK DAY!

The Crew were right.

The good-luck–bad-luck e-mails are mumbo jumbo.

I click the mouse button once.

Delete!

"Good news!" my mum says one morning.

I look up from my cereal and computer mag.

"Jay is coming to visit," she tells us.

I look up. "Cousin Jay, from New York?" I ask.

Mum nods. "He will be here for a week," she says. "He can share your room, Ravi."

Wait till I tell the Crew!

"So what's Jay like?" Amber asks.

"Dunno – I've never met him," I say.

Harvey shrugs. "Hey, he's a New Yorker – he's gotta be cool!"